Snakes

Rachel Firth and Jonathan Sheikh-Miller

Designed by Cristina Adami,
Nickey Butler and Neil Francis

Illustrated by John Woodcock

Edited by Gillian Doherty
Consultants: Chris Mattison and Kevin Buley
Managing editor: Jane Chisholm
Managing designer: Mary Cartwright
Photographic manipulation: Roger Bolton and John Russell

Contents

Internet links

Look for boxes like this where you will find descriptions of interesting Web sites about snakes. To visit the Web sites, go to Usborne Quicklinks at **www.usborne-quicklinks.com** and enter the keywords "discovery snakes". There, you will find links to all of the Web sites.

★ Many of the pictures in this book have a symbol like the one on the left. You can download these pictures from the Usborne Quicklinks Web site. For more information on using the Internet and downloading Usborne pictures, see inside the front cover and page 62.

This page: An eyelash viper
Title page: West African green mamba

What is a snake?

There are over 2,500 different species, or types, of snakes. They belong to a group of animals called reptiles. Snakes are very easy to recognize as they have distinctive long, thin bodies and no arms or legs.

In the family

This lizard, called a chameleon, is a relative of snakes.

Snakes are related to crocodiles, lizards and turtles, which are also reptiles. Reptiles have scaly skin and are "cold-blooded". This means that they do not have a constant body temperature. Snakes will often move between sun and shade to help warm themselves up or cool themselves down.

Where do snakes live?

Snakes live in a variety of places, or habitats. Most snakes live either on the ground or in trees. But some spend much of their time underground, and a number of snakes even live underwater, in rivers or in the sea.

This is a rough green snake. It lives in grass and bushes, but it also climbs trees and swims in streams.

Internet links

Go to **www.usborne-quicklinks.com** and enter the keywords "discovery snakes" for a link to a Web site where you can visit a reptile house at a zoo and see different types of snakes.

All over the world

Snakes are found in many parts of the world but are most common in warm tropical areas. This is because the heat helps to keep their body temperatures quite high. But snakes can survive in all kinds of places – in deserts, high up on cold mountain rocks and even within the Arctic Circle.

This Peringuey's adder lives in the sandy Namib desert in Africa.

This green palm viper lives in the tropical rainforests of Costa Rica.

All sorts of snakes

Although different kinds of snakes have similar body shapes, they don't all look the same. Some snakes can be five times as long as a person, while others are smaller than a person's foot. Snakes also have a wide variety of patterns on their skins.

Are snakes dangerous?

There are many different types of snakes, but most are harmless to humans. About 400 species have venomous, or poisonous, bites, but only a small number of these could cause serious injuries to people.

This eyelash viper has pointed scales above each eye, which make it look as if it has eyelashes.

Fact: Although snakes are found in most parts of the world, there are none in the wild in either Ireland or New Zealand.

Snake shapes and skeletons

Although you may not be able to tell at first glance, there are important differences in snakes' shapes. By looking at a snake's shape, you can often guess what kind of place it lives in.

Three shapes

Snakes' bodies have three main shapes. Round snakes often live underground. Their shape enables them to move easily through soil and sand. Some flat-bottomed snakes live in trees. Their shape helps them to grip onto rough surfaces, such as bark. Narrow snakes also often live in trees. Their shape helps them to stay rigid as they slither from one branch to another.

Here you can see the three main types of snake shapes in cross-section.

A narrow snake

A round snake

A flat-bottomed snake

This Asian long-nosed tree snake has a thin, light body which enables it to slither over these leaves without bending them.

Thick and thin

Some snakes are much thinner and lighter than others. Many of them live in trees and being light enables them to slither along small branches without breaking them. Others live in open country. They are fast movers and chase after animals for food.

Snakes that are short and thick, such as some vipers and pythons, are usually slow-moving and don't chase animals or climb trees.

Changing shape

Some snakes can change their shapes for a while. For example, European vipers can flatten their bodies. They do this when they are lying out in the sun. By making their bodies flatter, they expose a larger area to the sun. This means that they can soak up heat more quickly.

 Internet links

Go to **www.usborne-quicklinks.com** and enter the keywords "discovery snakes" for a link to a Web site where you can discover some of the advantages of being snake-shaped!

 Fact: Many snakes have only one working lung – their right lung. There isn't enough room inside their bodies for their second, much smaller, left lung to function.

Long organs

Although snakes' body shapes can vary, all snakes are long and thin compared to other animals. Snakes' inside organs, such as their hearts, stomachs, lungs and kidneys, are long and thin too. A snake's inside organs are protected by its skeleton.

This shows what the inside of a snake looks like.

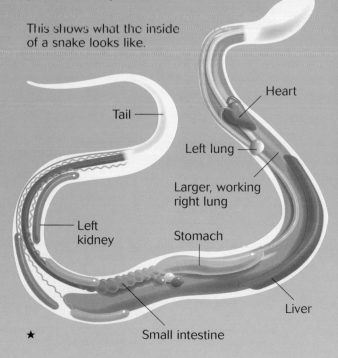

Tail

Heart

Left lung

Larger, working right lung

Left kidney

Stomach

Small intestine

Liver

★

Snake skeleton

A snake's skeleton is made up of a skull, a backbone and ribs. The backbone is made from lots of little bones called vertebrae. Snakes have more vertebrae than any other type of animal.

The dark area running down the middle of this snake's skeleton is its backbone.

Ribs are curved bones attached to a snake's neck and backbone. Snakes have between 150 and 450 ribs. These help to support the large amount of muscle a snake needs to move around and hunt.

Skin and scales

A[ll] snakes have scales covering their skin. These scales are of different shapes and sizes depending on where they are on the snake.

Head scales —

Ventral scales are on the underside of the snake.

Dorsal scales are in rows on the snake's back.

Subcaudal scales are under the snake's tail.

Smooth and rough

Many snakes have very shiny scales which make them look as if they're wet and slimy. In fact, if you touch a snake, it usually feels dry and smooth. But not all snakes are smooth and shiny. Puff adders, for example, have very rough, or keeled, scales which make them look dull and flaky.

These puff adder's scales are rough, or keeled.

These smooth scales are the dorsal scales of an emerald boa.

These are the dorsal scales of a ratsnake.

Protective scales

Scales form a protective shield around a snake's body. They are hard enough to stop some insects from biting snakes. They also help to prevent snakes from being badly wounded by animals that bite back as a snake attacks them.

This desert horned viper has two special scales behind its eyes that look like two little horns. Scientists aren't sure what they're for.

Keeping water in

Some snakes live in very hot, dry places, where most other animals couldn't survive. Snakes are able to live there because their scales help to keep moisture inside their bodies, stopping them from drying out. Like all animals, if snakes become too dry, they will die.

Internet links

Go to **www.usborne-quicklinks.com** and enter the keywords "discovery snakes" for a link to a Web site where you can read some fascinating facts about snakes and find out how their scales help them to move.

Shedding skin

When a snake's eyes become clouded, like this ratsnake's eyes, it is about to shed its skin.

Throughout their lives, as snakes grow bigger, they grow new skins. Every time they grow a skin, they have to shed the old one. They do this all at once, usually in one big piece. You can easily spot snakes that have recently shed their skin. Their new skin looks very shiny.

The snake begins to shed its skin by rubbing its snout on a rough surface to tear the skin.

Next it begins to wriggle out of the skin. As the skin is pulled off, it is turned inside out.

★

Once the whole skin is off, the snake can slither away, leaving it behind.

 Fact: Montpellier snakes and some sand snakes "polish" their scales with an oily liquid that comes out of their noses. Scientists aren't sure why they do this.

Slithering snakes

You might think that it would be difficult for snakes to move around without any legs. But, in fact, snakes can get around easily by slithering on their bellies. Indeed, they move in a variety of amazing ways.

S-shaped slithering

Most snakes move by pushing first one side of their bodies and then the other against small rocks or bumps on the ground. As they do this, their bodies form s-shapes. This is called serpentine movement. Snakes move in a similar way when swimming.

Here you can see how a snake pushes against small rocks on the ground to help it move forward.

This boa constrictor is moving along branches using s-shaped movements.

★

Sliding smoothly

Some large snakes appear to move along effortlessly in a straight line. They do this by tightening and then relaxing their muscles in waves down their bodies. As they do this, their scales grip onto any bumps on the ground, helping them to move along. This way of moving is known as rectilinear, or straight-line, movement.

This shows how a snake moves forward in a straight line. A snake might lift its head up as it moves to give it a better view.

Folding and stretching

When snakes are in narrow spaces, such as tunnels or burrows, they move by folding and then stretching their bodies. By bunching up one half of the body, until it is wedged between the sides of a tunnel, a snake can then push or pull the rest of its body forward. This is called concertina movement.

The snake squashes up its body so that it is tightly wedged against the walls of the tunnel.

Next the snake pushes the front half of its body forward.

Then the snake folds up the front half of its body so that it can pull the back half after it. ★

⊚⌒ Internet links

Go to **www.usborne-quicklinks.com** and enter the keywords "discovery snakes" for a link to a Web site where you can see a desert horned viper sidewinding across the Sahara desert.

Sidewinding in the sand

Many snakes find it difficult to move over smooth, loose surfaces, such as sand, because there is little to push against. But desert snakes have a special way of doing this. The snake makes a loop with its body, and then throws its head and the loop forward and to the side. By repeating this action, the snake is able to move sideways across the sand. This is called sidewinding.

As this African viper moves sideways, it leaves behind clear tracks in the sand.

Fact: Unlike many animals, snakes can't move backward. Instead, they have to turn around and slither back the way they came.

Snake senses

Snakes need very keen senses to hunt down food and avoid animals that hunt them. Although they have sight, smell, taste and touch, as we do, they also have some more unusual ways of detecting things in their surroundings.

Snake sight

Many types of snakes have very poor eyesight. For example, snakes that live in burrows underground have small eyes and can only tell the difference between light and dark. But some snakes have far better eyesight. They are good at detecting movement which helps them when they are hunting for animals to eat.

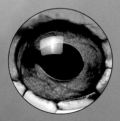

The black circle in the middle of this boomslang's eye is called a pupil. Snakes with such large, round pupils usually have good eyesight.

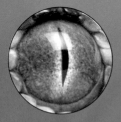

Snakes with slit-like pupils, like this white-bellied viper's, can usually see much better at night. In the dark, their pupils become larger.

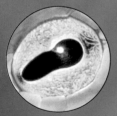

This is a green whip snake's eye. Scientists aren't sure whether its key-hole shaped pupil helps it to see better.

Detecting smells

Snakes can detect smells using their nostrils just as other animals can. But they also have special smell detectors, called Jacobson's organs, in the roofs of their mouths.

Jacobson's organ

Forked tongue ★

A snake can pick up tiny, invisible particles of scent from the air on its forked tongue. When it pushes its tongue over its Jacobson's organ, it can tell what the scent is. This means it can identify animals nearby, even if it can't see them.

Like all snakes, this grass snake can use its tongue to help it detect smells.

Detecting vibrations

Snakes' ears don't have outside openings as people's ears do and they can't hear many of the sounds that we hear. But they can detect vibrations in the ground made by other animals. When a snake has its lower jaw in contact with the ground, the vibrations travel through the bones in the snake's jaw to its ears.

Mysterious senses

Some snakes have small hollows and pimples on some of their scales. Scientists aren't sure what they are for. Some think that they are sensitive to light and tell the snake which parts of its body are exposed to light and which are safely concealed in the dark.

Heat seekers

Pit vipers, and some species of pythons and boas, are able to detect heat in a way that no other animal on earth can. They have little areas near their mouths called heat pits. All animals give off heat. If an animal approaches a snake, the snake can detect a change in temperature with its heat pits.

The open areas in this green tree python's face are its heat pits. With them, it can detect heat given off by other animals.

When a rabbit sits very still and is hidden by plants, it is very difficult for a snake to see it.

The snake is able to locate the rabbit because of the heat it gives off.

 Fact: Snakes' heat pits are so sensitive to temperature that they can detect changes of 0.002°C (0.0036°F), or even less.

Teeth, fangs and jaws ....

All snakes are predators, which means that they hunt animals for food. They eat their prey (the animals they hunt) whole, even if those animals are much bigger than they are. Snakes' jaws and teeth are specially adapted to help them eat in this way.

Sharp teeth

Some snakes have hardly any teeth and others have a lot. Snakes don't chew or tear at flesh with their teeth. Instead, they use them to grip their prey. Most snakes have extremely sharp teeth that point backward.

This brown house snake is using its teeth to pull its prey into its mouth.

This is the skull of a viper. You can see its teeth pointing backward into its mouth.

Fearsome fangs

Some snakes have two very sharp, long teeth called fangs. They use them to inject venom, a poisonous liquid, into their prey or, sometimes, into an animal that is threatening them. Once injected with venom, the animal usually dies.

Loose bones

Snakes that swallow large animals have stretchy skin, and skulls with bones that can move apart from one another. These allow them to open their jaws very wide, so that they can fit their prey into their mouths.

Internet links

Go to **www.usborne-quicklinks.com** and enter the keywords "discovery snakes" for a link to a Web site where you will find pictures of different venomous animals, including snakes, to paint online.

Fold-back fangs

When most snakes close their mouths, their fangs fit neatly inside their mouths, as people's teeth do. But some snakes, such as vipers, have very long fangs so they have to fold them backward into their mouths when they are not needed.

This puff adder belongs to the viper family. It is able to fold back its fangs because they have joints at the bases which work like hinges.

Rear-fanged snakes

Here you can see how far back in its mouth the fangs of a rear-fanged snake are.

Most snakes' fangs are at the front of their mouths, but a few snakes have fangs further back. This means that they have to open their mouths very wide to inject venom. If a rear-fanged snake's victim struggles, the snake will bite it again and again until it dies. This makes the snake look as if it is chewing the animal.

★

 Fact: After swallowing food, snakes appear to yawn. They do this to make the skull-bones that have moved apart slip back into their normal positions.

Hunting for food

Many predators chase after their prey when hunting, but this uses up a lot of energy. To save energy most snakes usually lie in wait for their victims. Some snakes also eat prey that is already dead, for example animals that have been run over on roads.

Lying in wait

Snakes usually lie in wait in places their prey often visit. They find these places by detecting the scents animals leave behind. A snake may have to wait many days before an animal comes close enough for it to seize it.

Going for the kill

When an animal finally gets close enough to a waiting snake, the snake suddenly thrusts forward and grabs the animal in its mouth. This is called striking.

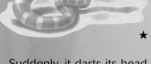

The snake spots prey and slowly bends its neck into a squashed s-shape.

Suddenly, it darts its head forward to catch the prey in its mouth.

★

First this eyelash viper lies very still, waiting for its prey, a tiny hummingbird, to come closer. When the bird is close enough, the viper strikes out. But this time, the snake isn't quick enough and the bird escapes.

Chasing prey

A few small, fast snakes do chase after their prey. Green parrot snakes chase tree frogs across the forest floor, relying on good eyesight rather than their sense of smell to detect their prey.

Following prey doesn't always mean moving fast. Some snakes eat snails. They find the snails by following the trail of slime they leave behind.

This ringed snail-eater is carefully watching its prey, a snail.

This snail can't move very quickly which makes it a very easy target for the ringed snail-eater.

Tempting tails

Some snakes tempt their prey to come close to them. Young copperheads have brown, patterned bodies, but the tips of their tails are yellow. To attract prey, they waggle their tails. Frogs and lizards mistake the moving tail for a caterpillar, and move close in the hope of catching their next meal. But it's the snake that catches and eats them.

★

A frog might not realize that it's near to a snake because the snake keeps its body very still as it waits for its prey to come closer.

Internet links

Go to **www.usborne-quicklinks.com** and enter the keywords "discovery snakes" for a link to a Web site where you can find out more about how different snakes hunt for prey.

Fact: Snakes hunt and eat a wide variety of animals including rats, birds and crocodiles. Some snakes even eat other snakes.

Deadly biters

About a sixth of all snake species kill their prey by biting them and injecting poisonous venom into them. They may also bite other animals if they feel threatened by them, to defend themselves. This is usually why people get bitten.

This venomous boomslang can kill humans with its venom.

Hognosed vipers like this one mainly eat frogs and mice. But they can still be dangerous to humans if they feel threatened.

Lethal venom

Snake venom usually has at least one of two main types of poison in it. One type causes paralysis, or stops an animal from being able to move. The animal dies because its heart stops beating. The other sort of poison destroys an animal's flesh from the inside.

Even if a mouse is able to run away, after it has been bitten by a snake, it will still die, because it has been injected with venom.

Strong poison

How poisonous venom is varies from one species of snake to another. Snakes that eat fast-moving animals usually have stronger venom, which kills animals more quickly. If a fast-moving animal is injected with weaker venom, it may be able to escape and run far away from the snake before it dies.

Quick strike

It's important for a snake to bite its victim quickly, so that the animal doesn't have the chance to fight or run away. An animal may not know that a snake is nearby until it has already been bitten. A snake usually checks carefully to make sure that its prey is dead before it eats it. The snake waits a while for the venom to take effect. It then flicks its tongue all over the animal's body.

This coral snake (the snake with a striped pattern) has made sure this crowned snake is dead and is now beginning to swallow it.

Swallowing food

A snake swallows its prey by moving each side of its jaw in turn to pull the animal down its throat. It uses its teeth to hook into the animal's body. Once the animal is in the snake's throat, strong muscles pull it further down into the snake's stomach.

Digesting slowly

As soon as an animal has been bitten, the snake's venom begins to digest it, or break it down, from the inside. In the snake's stomach, juices break the animal down even more. It can take many days for a snake to digest a big meal.

The snake grips a frog in its jaws and begins to swallow it head first.

The frog is in the snake's stomach. You can see its shape.

Now the frog has almost been digested.

Fact: Snake's venom is most effective on the type of animal the snake usually eats. Other animals may be less affected by the venom.

19

Suffocating snakes

Not all snakes kill their prey by injecting them with venom. Some of them kill animals by squeezing them until they stop breathing. These snakes are known as constrictors.

This anaconda is constricting a caiman (a reptile that's similar to an alligator).

Coiled killer

A constrictor kills its prey by coiling itself around the animal's body. The animal's lungs are then squeezed so that the animal can't take in air. When an animal dies because it can't breathe, this is called suffocation. Sometimes, the pressure of the snake's body stops the animal's heart from beating before it has suffocated.

Swallowing smoothly

If a snake is constricting a large animal, such as a crocodile, it can take several minutes for the animal to die. Once the animal is dead, the snake begins to swallow it whole. It will usually start with the animal's head. If the snake started at the tail end, the animal's legs would be pushed outward as it moved down the snake's throat, making it much more difficult to swallow.

After the snake has constricted its prey, it remains tightly coiled around it.

Next the snake begins to pull the animal head first through its coils and into its mouth.

★

As the snake swallows more of its prey, it begins to loosen its coils.

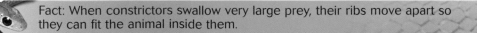

Fact: When constrictors swallow very large prey, their ribs move apart so they can fit the animal inside them.

Pushing pythons

Some constrictors, such as Australian woma pythons, hunt animals that live in burrows, often following them down into their burrows. Sometimes, there isn't enough room in a burrow for the snake to coil around its prey. Instead, it pushes the animal against the wall of the burrow until it can no longer breathe.

★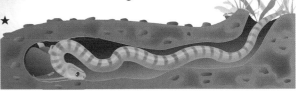

Here you can see how a snake suffocates its prey in a burrow by squashing it against the wall. There isn't enough room for it to coil around its prey.

Internet links

Go to **www.usborne-quicklinks.com** and enter the keywords "discovery snakes" for a link to a Web site with a fact sheet to print out about boa constrictors.

Swallowed alive

Some animals are difficult to kill by constriction. For example, frogs are difficult to constrict. When they are squeezed, they can make their lungs swell up, allowing more air to get into them. This makes it difficult for snakes to suffocate them. Constrictors either avoid eating frogs or swallow them live.

Heavy eaters

Snakes often eat animals that are much bigger than they are. Swallowing a big animal makes the snake very heavy, and it is unable to move very fast after such a large meal. If they are threatened in this state, they are able to bring back their food so that they can slither away more quickly.

A rock python swallowing an antelope

Camouflage and warnings ....

Some snakes are hard to see because the patterns on their skin allow them to blend in with their surroundings. This is called camouflage. Other snakes have bright skin which makes them easy to see. In different ways, both types of skin help snakes to avoid being attacked by predators.

Watch your step

In this picture, a carpet viper is partly buried in sand and so is fairly hard to see.

In Africa and Asia, carpet vipers kill a lot of people. These snakes are very hard to see because they blend in with the dry, rocky areas where they live. Often, people tread on them by mistake and are then bitten. Carpet vipers can also bury themselves by wriggling their bodies and this adds to their camouflage.

Lost in the trees

Many snakes that live in trees, such as the striped palm viper and the white-lipped pit viper, have green skin which helps them to keep well hidden among the leaves.

The vine snake also lives in trees, but looks very different from most tree snakes. This snake is thin and mainly light brown, just like a branch, or vine. When it is perfectly still, it is very hard to spot.

This vine snake can easily disappear from view in a large shady tree.

Fact: All snakes that are born totally white are called albinos. They find it very hard to hide and so become easy prey.

Snake warnings

Some venomous snakes have bright skin which makes them easy to see and warns attackers that they are best left alone. For example, coral snakes are highly venomous and have vivid skin patterns.

This blue Malayan coral snake has bright skin which warns predators that it is very venomous.

Mimicking milk snakes

Some harmless snakes also have bright skin patterns, so that predators think they are a venomous species and will leave them alone. In America, the skin patterns of harmless milk snakes closely resemble those of deadly coral snakes.

It isn't easy to tell which is the harmless snake and which is the venomous one.

Coral snake

Milk snake

Ringneck surprise

Ringneck snakes are able to change their appearance very quickly if they feel threatened.

Usually, a relaxed ringneck snake shows only its dark brown or black topside.

But a ringneck has a red tail which it reveals when it senses danger.

★

It also has a bright underside and it will roll over to show this if the danger persists.

Staying alive

Snakes are usually very shy and try to avoid trouble by hiding or moving away from danger. But if a possible attacker takes too much of an interest in them, some snakes are able to use unusual tactics to avoid being attacked.

Up for the challenge

When threatened, cobras raise the front parts of their bodies off the ground and stretch the skin on their necks to form a wide hood. To do this, they spread out the flexible rib bones in their necks, so that the skin tightens. They then look much bigger and more threatening.

A relaxed cobra lies flat on the ground, keeping its hood hidden.

When it senses danger, the cobra raises the front of its body and begins to stretch out its hood.

If alarmed, the cobra rises even further off the ground and spreads its hood defiantly.

This Indian cobra has risen up high and opened its hood to make itself look more intimidating.

Spitting with rage

Some cobras can spit jets of venom through small holes in the fronts of their fangs when they are threatened. They can hit predators as far away as 3m (9ft).

Cobras rise up off the ground before spitting and aim for the predator's eyes. If venom enters the eyes, it causes great pain and may badly damage eyesight.

This Mozambique spitting cobra is defending itself against a possible predator.

A warning rattle

Rattlesnakes get their name from the rattles at the tips of their tails. These are made of old scales that are left behind each time a snake sheds its skin.

When a rattlesnake vibrates its tail, the old scales rub together and make a rattling noise. The snake uses this as a way of warning animals to keep away.

Rattles are fragile and sections like this one often break off. They are soon replaced by more old scales, every time a snake sheds its skin.

Playing dead

This grass snake may look dead but it is very much alive and is trying to trick a possible predator.

When a predator is near, some snakes, such as grass snakes, turn over on their backs, stick out their tongues and lie very still, as if they are dead. They do this in the hope that the predator will then ignore them and move away.

 Fact: Some snakes emit foul smells when threatened. One species, the Chinese stink snake, gets its name from this unattractive habit.

Getting together ....

Snakes usually live alone. But occasionally they come together to breed, or produce young. All snakes breed by mating with another snake, apart from the brahminy blind snake which can produce babies all by itself.

These two smooth snakes are mating.

Finding a mate

In order to breed, the first thing most snakes have to do is find a mate (a snake of the opposite sex). Usually, it is the male snake that does the searching. When female snakes are ready to mate, they produce a strong smell. By following this smell, a male snake can track down a female.

Mating snakes

In order to produce baby snakes, one of the female snake's sex cells (eggs) has to join up with one of the male snake's sex cells (sperm). By becoming entwined with the female snake, the male snake is able to place some sperm in the female so that the cells can join together. The snakes may remain wrapped around each other for hours.

Fact: Some female snakes can store sperm inside them for several years, so that they can continue to have babies without needing to mate again.

Fighting for a female

Some male snakes, such as mambas, vipers and rattlesnakes, will fight with each other over a female snake. They rear up and wrap themselves around one another, each trying to push the other to the ground. The snake that wins may mate with the female snake, if she allows it.

These two male mambas may look as if they are being friendly, but in fact they are fighting over a female.

Snake ball

Some snakes don't have to look far for a mate. Large groups of red-sided garter snakes spend the cold winter months asleep in shared burrows. When they wake up, it is time to mate. Up to 100 male snakes all try to mate with the same few female snakes, forming a tangled "mating ball" around the females. Only one male will succeed in mating with each female in the mating ball.

Strange snakes

Brahminy blind snakes are very unusual because they are all female. Each female is able to develop eggs when she reaches adulthood, without needing to mate with a male snake. The eggs contain female snakes which are all exact copies of their mother.

This brahminy blind snake can produce babies without ever needing to mate.

Baby snakes

Some female snakes give birth to live young, but most lay eggs. Their growing babies stay inside the eggs until they are ready to break out, or hatch.

Safe inside

Snake eggs need to be kept at the right temperature, or incubated, for the baby snakes inside to grow and develop. Some female snakes bury their eggs in rotting leaves, or place them under rocks. This stops them from becoming either too cold or too hot.

These python's eggs are kept warm and protected by their mother as she coils around them.

Protective pythons

Although some female snakes stay near their eggs to warn off predators, most leave their eggs after they have laid them. Female pythons are unusual because they coil themselves around their eggs to protect them and incubate them.

Hatching out

About two months after a mother snake lays her eggs, the baby snakes are ready to hatch. Snakes' eggs aren't hard and easy to break like birds' eggs, but are more like strong paper. To hatch, baby snakes tear slits in their shells. They have a special tooth called an egg tooth to help them do this.

Baby snakes make tears in the tough, papery shells of their eggs.

A baby snake begins to slither through the hole in the egg.

★

The baby snake is able to slither off into the undergrowth immediately.

Keeping babies inside

Not all snakes lay eggs.
Some keep their eggs
inside their bodies, where
they are protected and
kept at the right temperature.
When the babies are ready to be
born, they break out of their eggs
while still inside their mother's
body. The mother then pushes
the babies out of her body.

A new-born
boa constrictor

Independent babies

As soon as they have hatched or been
born, baby snakes are able to do
most of the things adult snakes
can do. They know how to protect
themselves and find food without
being shown how by their parents.

A baby snake, such as this
baby green mamba, will
go back inside its shell,
after making the first slit,
if it senses danger.

Fact: Babies that are kept inside female snakes take up a lot of room. This means
that the mother snake can only eat small animals until the babies are born.

Giant snakes

Snakes vary greatly in size. Some are as small as a pencil, while others are as long as a car. But a few are even bigger than that. The very biggest, fattest and longest snakes come from the python and boa families.

Measuring snakes

Finding out the length of a snake isn't as easy as it might sound. Snakes tend to coil their bodies when they are picked up which makes it difficult to measure them. Even when they are dead, it is still hard to be accurate because dead snakes stretch very easily when handled.

The green anaconda these hunters are holding is 5.5m (18ft) long.

Green anacondas like this one can weigh up to 180kg (400lb). That's about the same weight as three adult women.

Getting bigger

Snakes don't stop growing when they become adults, as people do. They continue to grow throughout their lives, although they grow much more slowly as they get older.

Heavy anacondas

Green anacondas are members of the boa family and are the heaviest of all snakes. Their weight slows them down on dry land. But in swamps and rivers, it is supported by water. This means that they can swim much faster than they can slither, and so they spend much of their time in water.

Fact: The New York Zoological Society has offered a cash reward for anyone finding a reticulated python over 9.14m (30ft) long. So far, no one has claimed the reward.

Patterned pythons

The reticulated python is the longest snake in the world. It can grow up to 9m (29ft) long. It is called the reticulated python because it has a net-like, or reticulated, pattern on its skin. Reticulated pythons usually eat small to medium-sized animals, such as monkeys or deer. But occasionally, they attack and kill humans, and have even been known to eat them.

Rat catchers

The Burmese python is the third-longest snake, reaching lengths of 6m (20ft). It mainly eats rats and other pests, and so is usually a useful snake to have around. But it will also eat chickens, making it unpopular with farmers.

Internet links

Go to **www.usborne-quicklinks.com** and enter the keywords "discovery snakes" for a link to a Web site where you can find out more about giant snakes.

The patterns on this baby reticulated python make it difficult to see when it lies still among the leaves of a forest floor.

Boas and pythons ....

Boas and pythons are closely related to each other and both belong to an ancient family of snakes called the boids. There are 27 known species of pythons and 35 species of boas. All of them are constrictors.

This boa constrictor has a thick, muscular body which helps it to hang onto trees' branches.

Boa constrictors

Boa constrictors, or common boas, are perhaps the best-known snakes. They can grow to be as long as 3m (9ft). This may be why some people think of them as being dangerous to humans. But, in fact, they rarely attack people and certainly wouldn't try to eat anything as big as a person. Instead, they feed on birds and other small animals.

The pattern on this carpet python's skin helps it to stay hidden from predators.

Carpet pythons

Carpet pythons come from Australia. They live in a wide range of places, from dry deserts to tropical rainforests. They are called carpet pythons because of the striking markings on their skin which look a little like the pattern on an oriental carpet.

Green tree pythons

Green tree pythons live in rainforests. The adult is a stunning shade of bright green, with an irregular pattern of white and yellow blotches down its back. This pattern looks similar to the pattern light makes when it shines through trees.

Green tree pythons, like this one, sleep in trees during the day and hunt at night.

Internet links

Go to **www.usborne-quicklinks.com** and enter the keywords "discovery snakes" for a link to a Web site where you can see pictures of boas and find out more about them.

Turning green

Surprisingly, when green tree pythons first hatch out of their eggs, they are bright yellow or, much more rarely, red. After about a year, they turn green. Scientists aren't sure why this happens.

This baby rainbow boa has smooth, shiny scales which appear to shimmer as it moves.

Rainbow boas

Rainbow boas have striking, shimmering scales. They live in rainforests, hunting mainly at night, when they look for bats, mice and other small animals.

Countless colubrids

The colubrid family of snakes contains a huge number of different species. About half of all snakes belong to this family. Most colubrids are totally harmless but a few are venomous and have occasionally killed people.

Boomslangs

All rear-fanged snakes belong to the colubrid family. Most of these pose no threat to humans, but the boomslang is an exception. It has very strong venom and its fangs are near enough to the front of its mouth to bite into a human.

Although boomslangs can be dangerous, they are not usually aggressive. It is easy to tell if one becomes angry or alarmed, because it puffs up its throat.

Boomslangs are graceful movers that live in trees. They have distinctive large eyes and pointed snouts.

Airborne snakes

The five species of flying snakes are part of the colubrid family. Flying snakes can't actually fly but they can glide spectacularly from tree to tree, in the tropical rainforests where they live.

They launch themselves into the air and form their bodies into s-shapes. To help them glide more easily, they spread out their rib bones so that their bodies become flatter and wider.

Internet links

Go to **www.usborne-quicklinks.com** and enter the keywords "discovery snakes" for a link to a Web site where you can see exciting video clips of snakes flying through the air.

This picture shows a flying snake forming its body in an s-shape as it launches itself into the air.

Hungry for eggs

There is no mystery about what egg-eating snakes like to eat. Although they are very thin, these snakes can easily swallow eggs that are more than three times the size of their heads.

This egg-eater has its mouth full after raiding a bird's nest. An egg-eater will eat many kinds of birds' eggs.

When an egg-eater finds an egg, it wedges it firmly against its body and then starts to stretch its mouth over it.

Once the snake has managed to stretch its whole mouth over the egg, it uses pointed spines in its throat to puncture and crush it.

★

When the egg has been emptied of food, the egg-eater spits the crushed, flattened shell out.

Hungry for rattlers

Even though rattlesnakes are venomous, they are easy prey for certain kingsnakes. This is mainly because these snakes are not badly affected by their venom. Kingsnakes can overpower rattlesnakes and swallow them while they are still alive.

This Californian kingsnake is starting to eat a rattlesnake it has overpowered.

Cobras

Cobras are very distinctive-looking snakes. An alarmed cobra with the hood on its neck spread wide is a dramatic and intimidating sight. There are many different species of cobras, including the longest venomous snake in the world, the king cobra.

The king of snakes

The king cobra's head is as big as a man's hand and its body can reach about 6m (18ft) in length. When alarmed, a king cobra can look a person in the eye, if it raises the front part of its body off the ground.

Internet links

Go to **www.usborne-quicklinks.com** and enter the keywords "discovery snakes" for a link to a Web site where you can find lots of interesting facts about king cobras by clicking on a life-size picture of the snake's body.

Nest builders

King cobras are the only snakes to build nests to protect their eggs. Once a female king cobra has laid her eggs, she guards them until they hatch, 60 to 80 days later. King cobras are not aggressive, but they may attack if they feel that their nest is being threatened.

King cobras are fairly thin snakes and have narrower hoods than most cobras.

To make a nest, a female king cobra uses the loops of her body to drag dead leaves into a pile.

Once the nest is complete, the king cobra lays her eggs inside the pile and then rests on top of it.

Weaver eaters

Weaver birds build nests high up in trees away from predators, such as snakes. But these nests offer no protection against South African cape cobras. They can climb to the highest branches and force their way into these nests to feed on baby birds and eggs.

Weaver birds build nests with long entrances to try to stop snakes from getting in.

Back to front

When cobras become alarmed, they rise up off the ground and display their hoods. On the backs of their hoods, many cobras have markings known as eyespots because they look similar to eyes. It is thought that they have them to confuse predators. A cobra can quickly turn around and start to escape, yet still appear to be facing its attacker.

The Indian cobra is known as the spectacled cobra, because the shape of its eyespots looks like a pair of glasses, or spectacles.

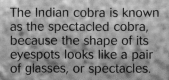

Fact: One bite from a king cobra contains enough venom to kill an elephant.

Sea snakes

M any snakes are good swimmers and will enter water to hide from a predator or to cool down on a hot day. But some snakes spend their entire lives in water. Some of these live in rivers and lakes, but most water-dwelling snakes are sea snakes.

Knotted snake skin

This shows how a sea snake twists its body to help it shed its skin.

Sea snakes shed their skin more frequently than land snakes. Some sea snakes, such as yellow-bellied sea snakes, rub their skin off by rubbing one part of their body against another. Their bodies look very tangled while they do this, and the skin they shed is often knotted into coils.

Coming up for air

Many sea snakes have to stay in water all their lives because they can't move on land and will soon die if washed up onto a beach. But sea snakes can't breathe underwater as fish can. Instead, they have to come up to the surface now and again to take a breath of air.

Once they have taken in enough air, most sea snakes can remain underwater for at least an hour. In fact, yellow-bellied sea snakes are able to hold their breath for over three hours.

Salty snakes

All animals need to drink water to survive. But the only water available to sea snakes is sea water, which is very salty.

Sea snakes can get rid of the salt they don't want using special organs under their tongues, called salt glands. Excess salt collects in the gland until the snake pushes its tongue out to smell. When the snake does this, salty water is pushed out at the same time.

Internet links

Go to **www.usborne-quicklinks.com** and enter the keywords "discovery snakes" for a link to a Web site where you can find out more about sea snakes and other venomous snakes.

This group of sea snakes is swimming together, looking for food.

Migrating snakes

Some sea snakes make long journeys together in large groups. This is called migration. In many countries there are legends about huge sea monsters. Perhaps what people really saw were hundreds of migrating sea snakes, moving along together. This may have looked like one huge animal.

Some people used to think there were huge snake-like monsters in the sea like the one shown here.

Deadly snakes

Sea snakes are among the most venomous snakes in the world. Belcher's sea snake is thought to have the most deadly venom. It is around a hundred times more venomous than the most venomous land snake.

In and out of the sea

Seakraits are distant relatives of sea snakes. They also live in the sea, but can leave it for dry land. They do this to mate and lay eggs. They also often move onto beaches to lie in the sunshine. The sun's warmth helps to break down food inside their stomachs more quickly.

This is a seakrait. It's not as well adapted to life in the sea as sea snakes are. But, unlike many sea snakes, it can move on land as well as in water.

 Fact: True sea snakes give birth to live young in the sea.

Mambas

Mambas are part of the same family as cobras. There are only four species of mambas and all of them live in Africa. Their highly venomous bites have made them both feared and respected by humans.

Green mambas are attractive snakes with bright green skin.

A gathering of greens

Several green mambas may live in one tree. But people hardly ever see them.

In some parts of Kenya and Tanzania, green mambas are found in very large numbers. Several hundred can live in an area about the same size as a small town park. Sometimes four or five can live in one large tree.

Green mambas

There are three different species of green mambas. They spend most of their time in woodland and forests where their green skin makes them very hard to see. Although they are highly venomous and have killed people, green mambas are not aggressive and prefer to move away from danger rather than attack.

 Fact: Without medical treatment, mamba bites can cause death within a few hours, or even just a few minutes.

Internet links

Go to **www.usborne-quicklinks.com** and enter the keywords "discovery snakes" for a link to a Web site where you can see pictures of other mambas and find out more about them.

Not so black mambas

Black mambas are rarely, if ever, black. They are usually a light chocolate-brown, but they get their name from the black lining of their mouths. Black mambas are the longest venomous snakes in Africa, reaching 4m (12ft) in length. They are also greatly feared because they are quite nervous and will attack if threatened.

Although black mambas spend much of their time on the ground, they are also good at climbing trees.

Fast snake

Black mambas are the fastest of all snakes, reaching speeds of 20kph (12mph) or more when they are on the attack. Even when moving quickly, they can keep their necks and heads off the ground, ready to make a sudden attack.

Home sweet home

Black mambas sometimes like to find a special place where they can regularly take shelter. They tend to choose holes in trees, rock crevices, and even the thatched roofs of houses.

More elapids

Cobras, sea snakes and mambas all belong to the elapid family. There are about 300 species of elapid snakes and many of them live in or near Australia. They vary greatly from one species to another. But one feature they all share is that they have highly poisonous venom.

Deadly taipans

Taipans are large elapid snakes that live in Australia and New Guinea. Inland taipans are the most venomous of all land snakes. A single bite from one would inject enough venom to kill 12 adult men.

Inland taipans, such as this one, are very dangerous to humans. But they are rare and few people have been bitten by one.

Death adders

Death adders don't belong to the same family as other adders (see pages 44–45). They are, in fact, another type of elapid. Like carpet vipers, they bury themselves under leaves, or in sand, to lie in wait for prey. This makes it easy to tread on them by mistake. Without fast treatment, a bite from a death adder can kill a person.

This northern death adder, like other death adders, is unusually heavy and wide compared to most other elapid snakes.

Fact: Death adders are unusual for elapids because they give birth to live young rather than laying eggs as other elapids do.

American corals

North, South and Central America are home to three different families of elapid coral snakes. Corals have striking bands of black, white, red and yellow all along their bodies. Although different corals eat different animals, they all eat other snakes, including snakes of their own species.

This is a coral snake. Coral snakes are quick to bite when disturbed. A person bitten by a coral snake should seek medical advice immediately.

Internet links

Go to www.usborne-quicklinks.com and enter the keywords "discovery snakes" for a link to a Web site about unusual tiger snakes that have survived on islands near Australia.

Australian tigers

Australian tiger snakes can be brown, black or olive green, with lighter bands across their bodies. Although there are other banded snakes known as "tiger snakes", only the tiger snakes of Australia are elapids. The ones that live in fairly cool areas are usually black. Dark things soak up more heat than light things. With their black scales, tiger snakes are able to keep warm in cold weather more easily than paler snakes can.

Black tiger snakes, like these two, are better able to survive in colder places than many other snakes.

Vipers and adders ......

There are over 200 different types of vipers (some of which are called adders) living all over the world. Many are well camouflaged and some are highly venomous.

Worldwide snake

The northern viper, or adder, lives in a wide range of places. It can be found in western Europe and Russia and it is the only snake living within the Arctic Circle. It is also the only venomous snake in Great Britain.

Adders, like this one, can tolerate cold conditions. This enables them to live in places where other snakes can't survive.

Sheltering snakes

During the winter months, adders hibernate, or rest, to avoid the cold harsh weather. When they do this, they sometimes group together in sheltered underground burrows or dens.

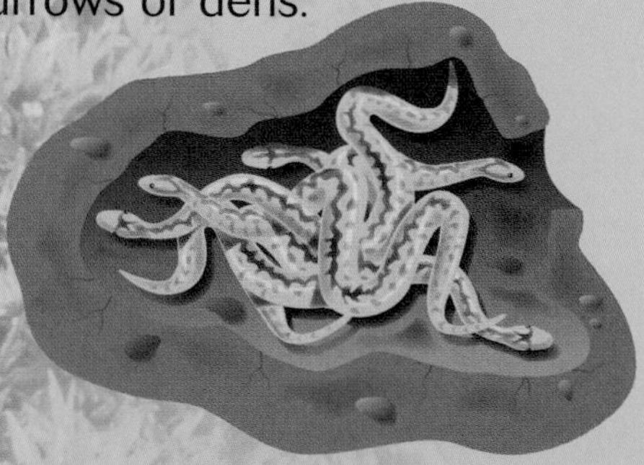

This picture shows a group of adders hibernating in an underground den.

Puffed-up snake

Puff adders get their name from their habit of puffing up their bodies when alarmed. They do this by quickly sucking in air. This makes them look bigger and more intimidating. As they let out the air, they make a loud hissing noise which is also meant to warn off predators.

A puff adder has a fat, chunky body and a flat, wide head.

When alarmed, a puff adder sucks in air and becomes even fatter.

⊚ ↝ Internet links

Go to **www.usborne-quicklinks.com** and enter the keywords "discovery snakes" for a link to a Web site where you can find facts and close-up photos of the common adder.

Patterned viper

The gaboon viper has brown, beige, white and black skin and is a very distinctive-looking snake. The patterns on its skin allow it to blend in with the floor of the tropical forests where it lives. It can conceal itself so well that even alert prey, such as monkeys, come close enough to be bitten.

This gaboon viper is partly hidden in a pile of dead leaves.

Pit vipers

Pit vipers are part of the viper family, but they have something in common with some boas and pythons – they have heat pits on their faces. This is how they get their name.

Heat pits

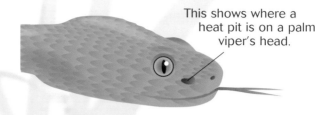

This shows where a heat pit is on a palm viper's head.

Cottonmouth

The cottonmouth is an aggressive and dangerous snake from the swampy areas in the southeast of the U.S.A. It gets its name from the skin inside its mouth, which reminds people of white cotton. Cottonmouths are easily angered, but luckily they give warning signals before they attack.

While boas and pythons have many heat pits on their heads, pit vipers have just two. They are located on either side of the snake's face, between its eyes and nostrils. Heat pits help pit vipers find prey if they are hunting at night.

This angry cottonmouth is trying to scare off a possible predator.

To scare off a predator, a cottonmouth opens its mouth and displays the white skin inside.

The cottonmouth also shakes its tail violently. If the predator doesn't move away, the snake may attack.

This fer-de-lance has caught a whiptail lizard and is injecting it with venom.

South American killer

The fer-de-lance belongs to a group of snakes called lanceheads. These snakes get their name from their triangular, pointed heads which look like the tips of lances, or spears.

The fer-de-lance lives in South America and is feared by workers on coffee and banana plantations. These deadly snakes hunt for rats and mice on plantations, and workers are sometimes bitten by them.

Internet links

Go to **www.usborne-quicklinks.com** and enter the keywords "discovery snakes" for a link to a Web site where you can see close-up pictures of fer-de-lance snakes.

Tail beaters

Bushmasters are large venomous snakes from the rainforests of Central and South America. To scare off predators, they beat the tips of their tails on dead leaves on the forest floor. This makes a loud rustling noise and warns animals to keep away.

A bushmaster snake coiled up on the forest floor

Fact: The Himalayan pit viper lives at 5km (3 miles) above sea level, in the Himalaya mountains in Asia. No other snakes live at such a height.

Rattlers

Rattlesnakes are one of the best-known species of snakes. They are part of the pit viper family and are only found in North, Central and South America. All rattlesnakes are venomous, and a few are potentially deadly to humans.

The Santa Catalina has one old scale on the tip of its tail instead of a rattle.

Getting rattled

When rattlesnakes sense danger, for example if a large animal is about to tread on them, they use the rattles on the ends of their tails to make a loud buzzing noise (see page 25). This warns nearby animals to keep away from them.

When a rattlesnake becomes alarmed, it raises its head off the ground and makes the front part of its body into an s-shape.

At the same time, the rattlesnake starts to shake its tail rapidly to make as loud a buzzing noise as possible.

★

Once the danger has passed, the rattlesnake lowers its head, stops vibrating its tail, and is able to relax once again.

Rattlesnake without a rattle

Santa Catalina rattlesnakes are the only rattlesnakes without rattles. On the island of Santa Catalina where these snakes live, there are no big animals, so they don't need rattles to warn them off. Without rattles they can also wait silently in bushes for lizards and birds to come close enough to bite.

Internet links

Go to **www.usborne-quicklinks.com** and enter the keywords "discovery snakes" for a link to a Web site where you can take a trivia quiz about rattlesnakes.

Fact: Rattlesnakes are greatly feared in the U.S.A., but, on average, they kill only 12 people a year. That's fewer than the number of people killed by lightning.

Deadliest rattlers

The aggressive mojave rattlesnake is the most venomous rattlesnake in North America, being almost twice as deadly as its nearest rival. The venom from just one of its bites could kill as many as 15,000 mice.

A few species of tropical rattlesnakes from South America, such as the cascaval, are even more deadly. They are known as "neck breakers" because a bite from one of them can cause a person's neck muscles to become rigid or frozen.

Mojave rattlesnakes live in rocky places and deserts.

Rattlesnake round-ups

These hunters are about to spray a jet of gas into a rattlesnake den.

In some parts of the U.S.A., people organize rattlesnake hunts, or round-ups. Hunters spray chemicals into burrows to drive snakes out into the open, where they are caught and then killed. The chemicals are very poisonous and kill many other animals living in the same habitat, such as foxes and skunks.

Underground snakes

Many species of snakes can burrow, or dig tunnels, and some spend most of their lives underground. The snake families with the largest number of burrowing snakes are blind snakes and thread snakes.

Bodies for burrowing

You might think that it would be difficult to dig without arms or legs. But burrowing snakes have developed special features to help them. They usually have perfectly round bodies and smooth scales, which help them move through soil easily.

Strong skulls

Many burrowing snakes have stronger, heavier skulls than other snakes. They need strong skulls to help them force their way through the soil.

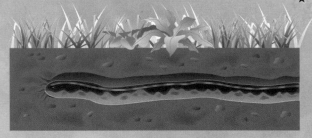

Strong skulls enable blind snakes to push their way through soil without hurting themselves.

Heads and tails

Some burrowing snakes, such as blind snakes, have heads that are the same shape as their tails. At first glance, it isn't always easy to tell which end is the head and which end is the tail.

Can you tell which end of this blind snake is its tail and which end is its head?*

*The snake's head is at the bottom of the picture.

This shiny-scaled sunbeam snake hunts other burrowing animals for food.

Borrowing burrows

Some snakes don't dig their own tunnels. Instead, they use ones made by other animals. They hunt underground for small burrowing animals, such as rats and even other snakes.

Short-sighted snakes

Most underground snakes have very small, simple eyes, compared to other snakes. They have poor eyesight and some may even be totally blind. But underground there isn't enough light to see by, so they don't need to have good eyesight. Instead, they rely on their sense of smell to help them find food.

This western thread snake has tiny eyes and very bad eyesight.

Occasional burrowers

Underground, snakes' eggs are better protected from predators than they would be on the surface.

Snakes that live mainly above ground also burrow from time to time. For example, ratsnakes and kingsnakes burrow if the temperature on the surface becomes too hot. Other snakes, such as pine snakes, make chambers underground and lay their eggs there.

 Fact: Some blind snakes can produce a smell which stops the ants they are hunting from trying to bite them.

Snakebite

Many thousands of people are bitten by snakes every year. However, normally this isn't because snakes are aggressive toward humans. Usually, they attack because they feel threatened.

Being bitten

If a person is bitten by a snake, it doesn't mean that he or she is going to die. Many snakes don't have any venom and some have venom that is too weak to hurt people very badly. Even so, anyone who is injected with any sort of snake venom will feel ill and will need medical treatment.

Carpet vipers, such as these, are responsible for many human deaths every year.

Warning bite

When venomous snakes bite people, they don't always inject venom. Every time a snake injects venom, it has to wait a while before it can inject some more. Instead of wasting venom on animals it can't eat, a snake will just sink its sharp fangs into an animal to warn it off.

Surviving snakebites

About fifty species of snakes inject venom that can kill humans. But a person will not usually die from a bite, if treated quickly. Scientists have developed medicine called antivenom, which is made from snakes' venom. If enough antivenom is given to someone soon after they have been bitten, they usually survive.

Different cures

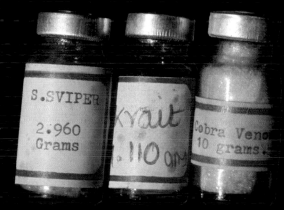

This carpet viper is being made to inject its venom into the jar. The venom will later be used to make antivenom.

The antivenom in these bottles can save the lives of people who have been bitten by snakes.

Because venoms from different snakes have different sorts of poisons in them, scientists have to make different antivenoms to treat different sorts of snakebites. So, if someone is bitten by a snake, it's very important to find out what sort of snake it was, so that doctors can give the patient the right antivenom.

Don't get bitten!

Of course, it's much better not to get bitten by a snake in the first place. Here are a few precautions you can take if you are walking in areas where there might be snakes:

- Leave snakes alone! If you leave them alone, they will leave you alone.

- Always cover up your legs and wear sensible shoes, and avoid walking through long grass.

- Never pick up a snake, even if it looks as if it is dead. It may just be injured or stunned, or even "playing dead".

 Fact: About 25,000 people die from snakebites each year.

Snakes at stake ....

Many people fear snakes because of their deadly reputations. But, in fact, snakes have more reasons to fear people. Snakes are hunted for their skin, their habitats are frequently destroyed, and many are killed by cars and trucks as they try to cross busy roads.

Threatened forests

Rainforests are home to many types of snakes, but millions of rainforest trees are cut down every year for their wood or to make way for farming.

As their habitats are wiped out, snakes suffer because their hiding places are destroyed and their prey is driven away. Snakes can't travel long distances, so they are unable to escape and many die.

Activities such as tree felling do vast amounts of damage to snakes' habitats.

Milos vipers are only found on a few Greek islands, including Milos, from which they get their name.

Skin trade

Over a million snakes are killed each year, so that their skin can be used to make handbags, wallets and boots. Some countries, such as India, have banned the exportation of snakeskin in order to discourage the hunting of snakes.

This snakeskin bag has a cobra's head on the front.

Snakes in danger

The numbers of some species of snakes are falling rapidly. For example, there are only about 2,500 Milos vipers left. They have been badly affected by the mining industry, forest fires and also by people running over them on roads. The Greek government is under a lot of pressure to help protect the Milos viper before it becomes extinct.

Road kill

Many snakes are killed by cars and trucks. This is because roads are often built through areas where snakes live. Most snakes are slow movers and find it hard to get out of the way of a fast-moving vehicle.

 Internet links

Go to **www.usborne-quicklinks.com** and enter the keywords "discovery snakes" for a link to a Web site where you can find out how to help protect the world's forests and the wildlife living in them.

 Fact: Since 1800, almost half of the world's total area of tropical rainforest has been destroyed.

 55

Rituals and legends

For many thousands of years, snakes have been viewed as mysterious, even magical, creatures. They have often been a part of ancient legends and tales, as well as religious rituals and beliefs.

Snake temple

Venomous Wagler's pit vipers, like this one, live around the pillars and statues of Penang's snake temple.

On the island of Penang, in Malaysia, there is an unusual Buddhist temple that is home to some deadly pit vipers. It was built in 1850 as a tribute to a respected local priest, who cared for snakes.

Local people say that on the day the temple was completed, a number of snakes came out of the jungle to live in the temple. These days, the temple is a tourist attraction and snakes are taken from the wild to keep it well stocked.

Snake monster

In ancient Greek mythology, there was a monster called Medusa, whose hair was made of real snakes. Just one glimpse of her face was supposed to turn a person to stone. According to the myth, she was killed by the hero Perseus, who chopped off her snake-covered head.

A sculpture of Medusa's head from a museum in Rome, Italy

Dancing with snakes

A Native American people called the Hopi think that snakes are messengers of the gods. Until recently, they used to hold nine day rituals, where they caught rattlesnakes and washed them. On the ninth day, they danced with the snakes, holding them between their lips. Then the snakes were released. The ritual was to ensure a good harvest and heavy rains.

This is a picture of one of the Hopi people wearing ceremonial clothing.

Charming snakes

Snake charming is an ancient but dangerous art. It involves a charmer playing a flute to a snake, often a deadly cobra, just a few feet away. As the charmer moves the flute from side to side, the snake sways to and fro, as if moving with the music. But as snakes have poor hearing, it is more likely to be following the movement of the flute because it thinks the flute may attack it.

Snake charmers, like this one, can be seen in India.

Fact: Most snake charmers look after their snakes, but some, afraid of being bitten, sew up the snakes' mouths or remove their fangs.

Snake facts ....

Snakes are intriguing animals and there is so much you can find out about them. Here are some fascinating facts for you to explore.

❧ The sharp-nosed viper is also known as the "hundred-pace snake". This is because it is said that a person can only walk 100 paces after being bitten by this snake before dropping down dead.

A deadly Russell's viper

❧ Russell's vipers are among the world's most dangerous snakes. Every year, their bites are responsible for the deaths of at least 10,000 people.

❧ The Antiguan racer is one of the world's rarest snakes. It is only found on small islands off the coast of Antigua in the Caribbean Sea. It is thought that there are fewer than 100 of these snakes in the wild.

A baby king cobra

❧ In parts of Asia, king cobras were once believed to be sun gods, who had power over the weather. Today, they are still highly respected there and are closely associated with the religions of Hinduism and Buddhism.

❧ The jumping viper from Central America gets its name from its habit of sometimes leaping almost 1m (3ft) off the ground when it launches an attack.

❧ Baby snakes have bites that are just as venomous as adult ones. In fact, because baby snakes are often much more aggressive than their parents, they can be particularly dangerous.

❧ All snakes have long, large stomachs. But some have stomachs that take up a third of the length of their bodies.

You may have noticed that snakes never blink. This is because they don't have eyelids. Snakes' eyes are protected from injury by a transparent, or see-through, scale.

In Haiti, a Caribbean country, one of the most important gods of voodoo religion is Damballa, a snake-god that lives in trees.

The gaboon viper has the longest fangs of any snake. They can be up to 5cm (2in) long.

Although you can't see it, this garter snake's eye is covered by a protective scale.

Some of the very first snakes were closely related to the boas and pythons of today. They lived 100 million years ago, when dinosaurs still dominated the Earth.

The Aboriginal people of Australia sometimes eat pythons. To cook a python, they roll it up into a coil and then cover it with clay before baking it over an open fire. Pythons are also eaten in Africa and the Far East.

You can clearly see the long fangs inside this gaboon viper's mouth.

After a good meal, some snakes may not need to eat again for a month. In fact, some large snakes, such as anacondas, are able to go for over a year without eating.

Glossary

This glossary explains some of the words you might come across when reading about snakes. Words in *italic* type have their own entries elsewhere in the glossary.

antivenom Medicine used to treat someone who has been bitten by a venomous snake. It can reverse the effects of *venom*.

aquatic Living in water.

arboreal Living in trees.

breed To produce young.

camouflage Markings on an animal's body that help it to blend in with its natural surroundings. These markings make it difficult to see the animal.

cold-blooded Having a body temperature that varies with the temperature of the surroundings. Cold-blooded animals are not able to produce their own body heat. They have to lie in sunshine to warm up.

concertina movement A way of moving along by bunching up the body and then stretching it out again. Snakes may move like this when they are in tunnels.

conservation Protection and preservation of our surroundings and the plants and animals living in them.

constrictor A snake that kills animals by squeezing them until they can't breathe any more.

egg tooth A special tooth which some baby animals have to help them break out of their eggs.

endangered Under threat. An endangered *species* is a type of animal or plant that is in danger of dying out.

environment The natural surroundings in which plants and animals live.

extinction When all the members of a *species* die out.

eyespot A marking which resembles an eye on the back of some cobras' heads.

fang A long, very sharp tooth. Snakes can use their fangs to inject *venom* into other animals.

front-fanged snake A snake with *fangs* near the front of its mouth.

habitat The place where a group of plants or animals lives.

hatch To break out of an egg.

heat pit An area near some snakes' mouths which is used to detect changes in the temperature of their surroundings.

herpetology The study of reptiles.

hibernate To sleep for a long period of time, often in the cold winter months.

hood A flap of skin covering cobras' ribs near their heads.

immune Resistant to a poison, such as venom, or a disease.

incubate To keep eggs at the right temperature for the babies inside to grow and develop.

Jacobson's organ A special organ in the roof of some animals' mouths which they can use to detect smells.

mate (noun) One of a pair of animals that *breed* together.

mate (verb) To come together to *breed*.

mating ball A tangled group of male snakes that are all trying to mate with a few female snakes.

migrate To make a long journey to look for food, or to find warmer surroundings.

predator An animal that hunts other animals for food.

prey An animal that is hunted for food.

protected species A type of animal that it is prohibited to hurt or kill because it is in danger of becoming *extinct*.

rainforest Very damp, hot forest, located in the *tropics*.

rattle Old scales at the tip of a rattlesnake's tail that make a sound like a rattle when the snake shakes its tail.

rattlesnake round-up An organized hunt for rattlesnakes.

rear-fanged snake A snake with *fangs* near the back of its mouth.

rectilinear movement A way of moving forward in a straight line.

reptile A *cold-blooded* animal with scaly, waterproof skin.

serpentine movement A way of moving by following an s-shaped path. Most snakes usually move in this way.

sidewinding A way of moving by repeatedly throwing the body to the side in a loop. Some desert snakes move like this.

species A type of plant or animal.

sperm Male sex cells.

strike To dart out to attack an animal.

subterranean Living mainly underground.

suffocate To stop an animal from breathing until it dies.

tropics Warm, wet areas, near to the Equator, an imaginary line around the middle of the Earth.

venom A poisonous liquid that some snakes inject into their prey.

warm-blooded Having a body that is able to produce its own heat. Animals that are warm-blooded can keep warm, even if their surroundings are cold.

Using the Internet ....

Most of the Web sites listed in this book can be accessed with a standard home computer and a Web browser. This is the software that enables you to display information from the Internet.
We recommend:

• A PC with Microsoft® Windows® 98 or later version, or a Macintosh computer with System 9.0 or later, and 64Mb RAM
• A browser such as Microsoft® Internet Explorer 5, or Netscape® 4.7, or later versions
• Connection to the Internet via a modem (preferably 56Kbps) or a faster digital or cable line
• An account with an Internet Service Provider (ISP)
• A sound card to hear sound files

Extras

Some Web sites need additional free programs, called "plug-ins", to play sounds, or to show videos, animations or 3-D images. If you go to a site and you do not have the necessary plug-in, a message saying so will come up on the screen. There is usually a button on the site that you can click on to download the plug-in. Alternatively, go to **www.usborne-quicklinks.com** and click on **Net Help**. There you can find links to download plug-ins. Here is a list of plug-ins that you might need:

RealPlayer® – lets you play video and hear sound files
Quicktime – enables you to view video clips
Flash™ – lets you play animations
Shockwave® – lets you play animations and interactive programs

Help

For general help and advice on using the Internet, go to **Usborne Quicklinks** at **www.usborne-quicklinks.com** and click on **Net Help**. To find out more about how to use your Web browser, click on **Help** at the top of the browser, and then choose **Contents and Index**. You'll find a huge searchable dictionary containing tips on how to find your way around the Internet easily.

Computer viruses

A computer virus is a program that can seriously damage your computer. A virus can get into your computer when you download programs from the Internet, or in an attachment (an extra file) that arrives with an e-mail. We strongly recommend that you buy anti-virus software to protect your computer and that you update the software regularly. For more information about viruses, go to **Usborne Quicklinks** and click on **Net Help**.

> For quick and easy access to all the Web sites in this book, go to **www.usborne-quicklinks.com** and enter the keywords "discovery snakes"

*Macintosh and QuickTime are trademarks of Apple Computer, Inc., registered in the US and other countries. RealPlayer is a trademark of RealNetworks, Inc., registered in the US and other countries.
Flash and Shockwave are trademarks of Macromedia, Inc., registered in the US and other countries.*

Index ....

Words with several pages have a number in **bold** to show where to find the main explanation. Page numbers in *italic* show where to find pictures.

Acknowledgements ....

Every effort has been made to trace the copyright holders of the material in this book. If any rights have been omitted, the publishers offer to rectify this in any subsequent editions following notification. The publishers are grateful to the following organizations and individuals for their permission to reproduce material (t=top, m=middle, b=bottom, l=left, r=right):

Cover © Joe McDonald/CORBIS; **p1** © Chris Mattison; **p2** © Michael & Patricia Fogden; **p4** (tl) © Chris Mattison, (m) © Steve Kaufman/CORBIS; **p5** (tl) © Michael & Patricia Fogden, (tr) © Michael & Patricia Fogden/CORBIS, (b) © Kevin Schafer/CORBIS; **p6-7** (t) © Michael & Patricia Fogden/CORBIS; **p7** (br) © The Purcell Team/CORBIS; **p8** (l) © Michael & Patricia Fogden/CORBIS, (tr) © Chris Mattison, (mr) © Chris Mattison, (br) © Chris Mattison; **p9** (t) © Steve Kaufman/CORBIS, (ml) © Chris Mattison; **p10** © Kennan Ward/CORBIS; **p11** © Carol Hughes/Bruce Coleman; **p12-13** © Colin Varndell/Bruce Coleman; **p12** (t) © Chris Mattison, (m) © Chris Mattison, (b) © Christer Fredriksson/Bruce Coleman; **p13** © Joe McDonald/CORBIS; **p14** (t) © Chris Mattison, (ml) © Rod Patterson; Gallo Images/CORBIS; **p15** © Andrew Bannister; Gallo Images/CORBIS; **p16** (t) © Michael & Patricia Fogden, (b) © Michael & Patricia Fogden; **p17** © Michael & Patricia Fogden; **p18** (t) Ardea/Chris Harvey, (b) © Michael & Patricia Fogden; **p19** © Michael & Patricia Fogden/CORBIS; **p20-21** Martin Wendler/NHPA; **p21** Fritz Polking/Still Pictures; **p22** © Michael & Patricia Fogden/CORBIS; **p23** (t) © Chris Mattison, (ml) © Michael & Patricia Fogden/CORBIS, (br) © Chris Mattison; Frank Lane Picture Agency/CORBIS; **p24** © David A. Northcott/CORBIS; **p25** (t) © Digital Vision, (mr) © George McCarthy/Bruce Coleman, (b) © Chris Mattison; **p26** Tony Phelps/BBC Natural History Unit; **p27** (t) Ardea/Adrian Warren, (b) © Chris Mattison; **p28** © Chris Mattison; **p29** (t) Brian Kenney/Planet Earth Pictures, (b) Anthony Bannister/NHPA; **p30-31** Telegraph Colour Library/Brian Kenney; **p30** © Jeffrey L. Rotman/CORBIS; **p31** © Michael & Patricia Fogden; **p32** (t) © David A. Northcott/CORBIS, (b) © Joe McDonald/CORBIS; **p33** (t) © David A. Northcott/CORBIS, (b) © Chris Mattison/Frank Lane Picture Agency; **p34** © Michael & Patricia Fogden; **p35** (t) © Michael & Patricia Fogden, (b) © David A. Northcott/CORBIS; **p36-37** (background) © Michael Freeman/CORBIS; **p36** © Rod Patterson; Gallo Images/CORBIS; **p37** (t) © Michael & Patricia Fogden, (m) © Robert Gill; Papilio/CORBIS; **p38-39** © Brandon D. Cole/CORBIS; **p39** © Stephen Frink/CORBIS; **p40** Joe McDonald/Bruce Coleman; **p41** © Joe McDonald/CORBIS; **p42** (r) © Michael & Patricia Fogden/CORBIS, (lm) © Terry Whittaker/Frank Lane Picture Agency; **p43** (t) © Michael & Patricia Fogden/CORBIS, (b) © John Cancalosi/Bruce Coleman; **p44** © George McCarthy/CORBIS; **p45** © David A. Northcott/CORBIS; **p46** © Joe McDonald/CORBIS; **p47** (t) © Michael & Patricia Fogden/CORBIS, (b) © Michael & Patricia Fogden/CORBIS; **p48-49** © David A. Northcott/CORBIS; **p48** © Chris Mattison; **p49** Jeff Foott/BBC Natural History Unit; **p50-51** © Chris Mattison, (background) © Michael & Patricia Fogden; **p50** © Michael & Patricia Fogden; **p51** © Michael & Patricia Fogden; **p52** © Jeffrey L. Rotman/CORBIS; **p53** (t) © Jeffrey L. Rotman/CORBIS, (m) © Jeffrey L. Rotman/CORBIS; **p54** Mark Edwards/Still Pictures; **p55** (t) © Chris Mattison, (b) Ardea/P. Morris; **p56** (t) © Joe McDonald/CORBIS, (l) © Araldo de Luca/CORBIS; **p57** (t) © CORBIS, (b) © Joe McDonald/CORBIS; **p58-59** © Joe McDonald/CORBIS, (background) © Chris Mattison; **p58** (t) © Chris Mattison, (l) © Joe McDonald/CORBIS; **p59** © Joe McDonald/CORBIS

With thanks to U.S. expert Rusty Gimpe.